Answering the Cry for Help

A Suicide Prevention Manual
for Schools and Communities

by Dave Opalewski, M.A. CTS

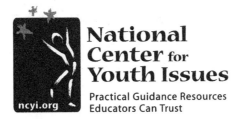

National Center for Youth Issues

Practical Guidance Resources
Educators Can Trust

P.O. Box 22185 • Chattanooga, TN 37422-2185
423.899.5714 • 800.477.8277
Fax: 423.899.4547 • www.ncyi.org

P.O. Box 22185
Chattanooga, TN 37422-2185
423.899.5714 • 800.477.8277
fax: 423.899.4547
www.ncyi.org

ISBN: 978-1-931636-73-5
© 2008 National Center for Youth Issues, Chattanooga, TN
All rights reserved.

Written by: Dave Opalewski, M.A.
Photography, cover and interior layout design by: Jacquelyn D. Kobet
Published by: National Center for Youth Issues

Printed in the United States of America

Mission Statement

Recognizing strength in unity, it is our purpose to help schools and communities work together to provide effective and appropriate programs and support systems to prevent suicide within the community. This will be accomplished by raising awareness through education and providing activities, training and support.

Adolescent suicide is not just a school issue, it is a community issue. It is our belief that the most effective preventative programs take place in communities where multiple agencies are involved and working together. These agencies consist of schools, churches and organizations such as Lions Club, community coalitions, counseling agencies, community mental health, etc. It is of paramount importance that education and support are available for all age groups within the community as well as adolescents.

Suicide is **NOT** about death
Suicide is about **ending pain**!

Table of Contents

Forward

In September of 1972, I began my career as an educator with determination that was second to none, and the usual idealistic and healthy views most beginners have. Shortly into this first year, however, I learned firsthand how difficult this world could be for our youth.

A boy we will call Bob, who I came to know through JV Football, came into my empty classroom at 3:20 in the afternoon after school dismissed for the weekend. He startled me as I was rushing to get my papers together so I could make a quick exit for the weekend. I asked, "Bob, what can I do for you?" He replied "nothing." When I asked him "Why are you here?", he replied, "I thought we could talk sometime." I told him we could talk any time, as I put student homework papers into my brief case and reached for my coat. To my surprise, Bob had a confused look on his face. I then asked him if there was anything else and he said "No" and left. That weekend Bob taped a shotgun to his mouth and pulled the trigger.

I was devastated. I felt responsible for what had happened. I beat myself up for a long time. I should have known that the time Bob wanted to talk was right then and there.

The very next year I had a boy I will call Sam on my JV Football team. Sam was a 4.0 student. He had two older siblings going to high profile colleges, and his parents both had administrative jobs at large corporations and were highly esteemed in the community. One weekend, Sam was out with some friends and like many teens, had a weak moment. He engaged in some unlawful behavior and was caught by the police. This incident (which would be considered minor in most circles) brought embarrassment to him and his family. In the following months Sam became introverted. He did not dress as neatly as he once did, and his over-all appearance declined. Sam ended up asphyxiating himself in his parent's garage.

All schools and communities have their Bobs and Sams. The risk that one or more of your students/adolescents will complete a suicide or attempt suicide is greater today than ever before. Yet we are still largely *reactive* instead of *proactive* in our approach to the problem. Also, many of the times we react, we do so in ways that are questionable. Many schools, even today, don't honestly acknowledge the suicide for fear that copycat behaviors might happen. Many schools also use outside counselors to try to "fix" the problem. Although outside resources can be of strong support, all of my research clearly indicates that the people that the students want to talk to when this tragedy happens are the people they see in school everyday and with whom they already have established relationships. They emphatically state that they don't want to talk to strangers.

It is estimated that we have over 5 million Americans who are "victims" of a loved one's suicide. [1] Chances are that some of those 5 million Americans are students or staff members in your school. Most people are not aware that grief from suicide has different dynamics than grief from death by other causes. In my experience, many of these "victims" carry tremendous guilt and pent-up anger. As an educator, I should have been trained as to what to look for in the cases of Bob and Sam. There are other issues as well that these "victims" go through, and they are discussed in later chapters.

Many times when schools do recognize this problem, they tend to approach the issue from within the school environment only, and they don't utilize the help and support of the rest of the community. One of the objectives of this work is to suggest ways schools can coordinate with the community and work together in a unified effort toward suicide prevention. It is my belief that this is the most effective method in developing an effective suicide prevention program.

Every year it is estimated that in excess of 100,000 people in the United States end their lives by suicide. These people are not just statistical numbers but are husbands, wives, mothers, fathers, sisters, brothers, children, friends and/or classmates. Whether we are survivors, or the supporters of survivors, we must learn how to deal with the debris of the tragedy. We must also take a proactive approach in the area of suicide prevention. This work attempts to help you do both.

Chapter **1**

S.O.S. –The Call Goes Out
Understanding the Need for Intervention

Chapter One

S.O.S. –The Call Goes Out
Understanding the Need for Intervention

According to the Center for Disease Control in Atlanta, suicide is the third leading cause of death among United States teens in the present age. [2] It is important to state here that these are the suicides we know about. Many experts claim that the number of suicides is more accurately 3 or 4 times greater than reported. In my short experience working in a funeral home, I quickly learned that if a suicide can possibly be called an accident, it will be. There are several reasons as to why this is so, but it is not my intent to discuss these reasons in this work. The Michigan Department of Community Health reports that in the year 2005, there were 4,212 known suicides in the 15-24 age group. [3] More disturbing is that if we multiply this number, as experts suggest, suicide would actually move up to the number two cause of death for this age group.

Until the 1960's suicide rates generally increased in direct proportion with age, with the lowest incidents among the young, and the highest incidents among the aged. Today, teens have the second highest rate of suicidal attempts to completions, second only to those 65 and older. [4]

Edwin Schneidman, one of our country's foremost suicidologists, states that, "There may be as many as 250,000 young people attempting suicide each year in the United States and perhaps a million more moving in and out of suicidal crisis, thoughts, and episodes." Schneidman also states that "There are an estimated 5 million Americans who are survivors of a loved one's suicide." [5] Chances are that some of these 5 million Americans are students in your schools and communities. We will address the perceptions and grief process of these "victims" in a later chapter.

Some additional statistics compiled by the Michigan Association of Suicidology are as follows:

- *Suicide is a thought common to 62% of U.S. adolescents.*
- *From 1994 to 2004 suicide increased 120% among middle school students.*
- *Each suicide completed affects at least 6 other people not including schoolmates.*
- *Whereas suicides account for 1.4% of all deaths in the U.S. annually, they comprise 14% of deaths of all people less than 25 years of age.*
- *Within a typical classroom, it is likely three students (one boy and two girls) have made a suicide attempt in the last year.*
- *Up to 60% of high school students report having suicide ideation.*[6]

Risk by Gender

Until the 1990's, teen male suicide attempts and completions were far greater in number than those of females. However, at the present time, there are more female attempts but more male completions. According to the National Association of Suicidology, "For every nine female attempts, there is one completion. For every four male attempts, there is one completion." The following two graphs are provided for your information. [7]

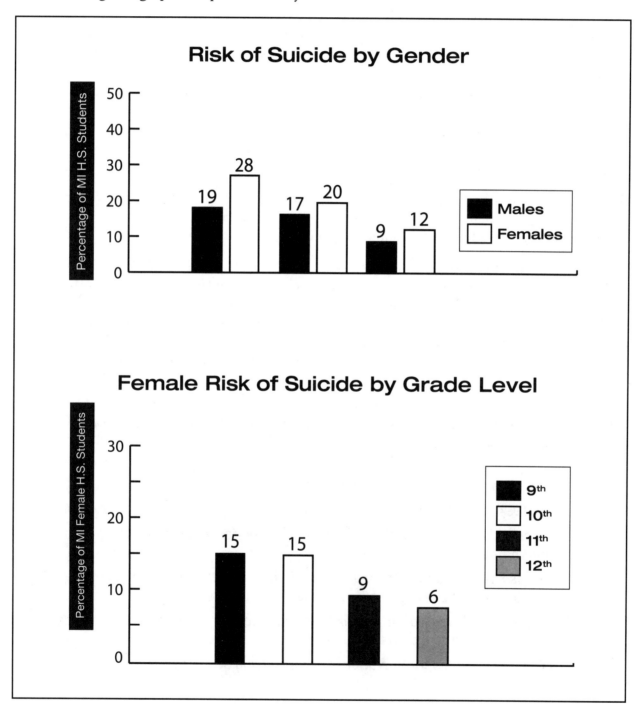

Answering The Cry for Help
© National Center For Youth Issues • www.ncyi.org • 1-800-477-8277
Please refer to page 2 for duplication information

Why Do Most Schools and Communities *NOT* Have Teen Suicide Prevention Programs?

The subject of suicide is a very fearful one indeed. As a Death Educator, my research identifies six reasons schools and communities do not have suicide prevention programs as a result of this fear.

- *I'm the only one in my school or community who is willing to learn about suicide.*
- *What if I don't diagnose the student at risk?*
- *What if I misdiagnose the student at risk?*
- *My administrator is afraid to deal with suicide.*
- *Won't discussing suicide with a suicidal student push them over the edge?*
- *The community doesn't acknowledge that teen suicide is a problem.*

In response to the first bullet point, I have found in my experience that it only takes one passionate person to get the project started. As far as the next two points, our job is *not* to diagnose but to give hope and support. We leave the diagnosing to the medical professionals. School administrators have a multitude of pressures in running their schools. It must be stressed to them that this problem doesn't just go away. It must be addressed. Discussing suicide with a student in crisis has proven to be a very effective preventative measure, if not the *most* effective preventative measure. In the several hundred school assemblies I have presented on suicide prevention, students have overwhelmingly stated to me that the most important statement I made was that "they want to talk about it."

The risk that one or more of your youths will complete suicide is greater today than ever before. Every year parents, teachers, and friends are shocked by the suicide of someone who did not match their concept of the "suicidal person." Documentation has shown that this is all too common. In most cases, something could have been done to save these lives.

We also have to recognize that we are all vulnerable. Although strong family structures are a deterrent, suicides can and do happen in good families as well. It is known that brain chemical imbalances which cause depression can be genetic. This depression may manifest itself as suicidal behavior. ***Whenever we feel we are not vulnerable, we become vulnerable.***

As a school teacher, counselor, administrator, or community activist, you are in the position to recognize potentially suicidal adolescents. You are also in the position to take action to help these young people who cannot or will not ask for help from their friends and family.

It is my intent to help you make a positive difference in the lives of adolescents in your community by helping you to:

- *Recognize causes of suicide*
- *Assess suicidal risk*
- *Take general steps to help the student*
- *Encourage parental and community involvement*
- *Understand the suicidal person*
- *Recognize and facilitate healthy grief after suicide*

Fact or Myth?

When dealing with the issue of suicide, it is best to separate fact from fiction. The following is a list of facts and myths about suicide compiled by Sol Gordon in his book, "When Living Hurts."

Myth: Youth who talk about suicide rarely attempt it.
Fact: Most youth that attempt or complete suicide, have given verbal clues.

Myth: Discussing suicide issues will make it happen.
Fact: Talking about suicide does not place ideas into young people's heads that were not already there. There is evidence that once a suicide occurs other attempts may follow as a contagious reaction to hopelessness.

Myth: The tendency towards suicide is inherited.
Fact: There is no evidence of a genetic link. However, a previous suicide in the family may establish a destructive model for dealing with stress and depression.

Myth: Teenage suicides happen at night.
Fact: Most teenage suicides occur between 3 and 6 PM, at home, presumably when the suicidal person can be seen and stopped.

Myth: Suicidal people leave notes.
Fact: Only a small percentage, about 15% leave notes.

Myth: If a person wants to complete suicide nothing can stop him/her.
Fact: Suicidal people have mixed feelings about death. They send out messages and clues that ask others to save or help them. No one is suicidal all the time. Many suicides can be prevented.

Myth: Youths who want to complete suicide are mentally ill.
Fact: Mental illness can increase the risk of suicide but most young people who attempt or complete suicide would not be diagnosed as "mentally ill." Youth suicide is often a sudden and urgent reaction to cumulative events and stresses.

Myth: Once a teenager has been suicidal, he/she is never out of danger.
Fact: Many youths that have been depressed recover and lead normal healthy lives. They learn constructive rather than destructive ways to cope and handle feelings and disappointments. [8] You can make a difference. In many schools and communities it is not a matter of whether you can or cannot, it is a matter of whether you will or will not.

Answering The Cry for Help
© National Center For Youth Issues • www.ncyi.org • 1-800-477-8277
Please refer to page 2 for duplication information

End Notes – Forward and Chapter One

1.   Scneidman, E. "The Suicidal Mind," Oxford University Press, June 1, 1996. New York, N.Y.

2.   National Center for Health Statistics Centers for Disease Control and Prevention 2007, Atlanta, GA

3.   Mich. Depart. of Community Health, Suicide Statistics, 2006.

4.   National Center for Health Statistics Centers for Disease Control and Prevention. 2007. Atlanta, GA

5.   Scneidman, E. "The Suicidal Mind," Oxford University Press, June 1, 1996. New York, N.Y.

6.   Michigan Association of Suicidology, Oct. 2003 Newsletter, Lansing, MI

7.   Mich. Dept. of Education, Michigan Assessment for Students at Risk, 2006

8.   Gordon, S. "When Living Hurts," Dell Books, Feb. 1989, New York, N.Y.

Chapter 2

Intercepting the Call for Help
**Recognizing Specific Risk Factors
for Potential Suicide**

Chapter Two

Intercepting the Call for Help
Recognizing Specific Risk Factors for Potential Suicide

Suicide is usually *not* a result of one or a few isolated events in an individual's life, but the end of a series of frustrating events.

The Main Causes

- *Substance abuse – alcohol or other drugs*
- *The break-up of the family*
- *Depression – caused by environmental or genetic factors*
- *Feelings of insecurity*
- *Illness*
- *Broken love affairs*
- *Economic conditions – poverty or wealth*
- *Disfiguring injuries or disease*

* *Many times, the person in crisis has 3 or more of the factors listed above.*

Behavioral Clues That a Person May Exhibit

- *Previous threats or attempts of suicide – It has been my experience in working with suicidal teens that each attempt seems easier for the teen and is more serious.*
- *Support for suicide from important role model (rock star, actor)*
- *Close friend or family member who attempts/completes suicide*
- *Feelings of failure – "I can't do anything right"*
- *Radical personality changes – persistent sadness; loss of interest in activities the person was once passionate about*
- *Withdrawal – from family, friends, and regular activities*
- *Noticeable changes in eating or sleeping habits*
- *Neglect of personal appearance*
- *A decline in the quality of school work*
- *Violent or rebellious behavior*
- *Alcohol or other drug use*
- *Verbal hints – "I won't be a problem for you much longer."*
- *Giving away prized possessions*
- *Suddenly becomes cheerful after a prolonged depression – The final decision may have been made, which is in itself a form of relief.*

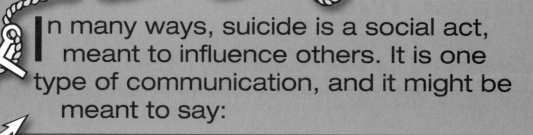

In many ways, suicide is a social act, meant to influence others. It is one type of communication, and it might be meant to say:

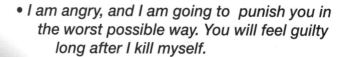

- *I am angry, and I am going to punish you in the worst possible way. You will feel guilty long after I kill myself.*

- *You never paid attention to me. No one has ever paid attention to me. But if I kill myself, you will have to pay attention to me.*

- *I need help, but I am not able to ask for it. I don't know how to ask for help. This is a way to ask for help.*

- *The pain of my life is too great. I can't stand it any longer. Either someone has to help me out of this pain, or I will help myself out by dying.*

- *I want to control you; I can do that by attempting suicide. I will be the victim and you will be the rescuer.*

The above list, although incomplete, may give you an idea of what the potential suicidal person may be thinking. Many times when we are familiar with what and how a person thinks, we can be more helpful in dealing with the person.

Expectations

Each of us has expectations for certain behaviors, performances or methods of handling situations. These are largely shaped by social, familial, religious and environmental factors. Expectations can be realistic or unrealistic. Often adolescents develop unrealistic expectations in their athletic, academic or maturity levels. Unrealistic expectations can also be the result of parents, educators or others not recognizing individual differences in children. Unrealistic expectations increase stress levels, the use of alcohol or other drugs, and potentially the risk of suicide.

Answering The Cry for Help

Young people today are under a great deal of pressure from the media about dating relationships, how to look, and what they need to have to be viewed as successful in life. This pressure from the media many times is contrary to the values of their family, and is most often unrealistic.

Also, the recent educational legislation seems to have added additional pressures for our youth. As an educator since 1972, I feel qualified to question the age appropriateness of many state education standards and benchmarks. When these standards and benchmarks are not age appropriate, students fail to see the relevance in their education and become frustrated. They see a bleak future for themselves. Also, when schools are "graded" solely on state assessment tests, discussion of important social and emotional issues tends to be less of a priority. A professor originally from China recently visited me in my office at Central Michigan University. He expressed to me his concern over the United States attempting to emulate China's educational system. According to Psychology Today July/August 2008 edition, "This culture of pressure and frustration has sparked a mental health crisis for young Chinese." The article goes on to state that "a disturbing number decide to end it all; suicide is now China's leading cause of death for those aged 20 to 35. People in China, especially parents of young students are suddenly becoming aware of huge depression and anxiety problems in young people."[1] Most disturbing is that we are trying to copy this educational system.

Changes in Perception

The foundation for our change in perception or our belief about what is true or what is happening is directly related to brain chemistry. An altered brain chemistry alters perception.[2] For example, if we have a lower than optimal level of serotonin (a chemical that regulates mood, appetite, body temperature and more), our brain may interpret uncontrollable situations negatively and therefore, we take them personally. The weather may be taken personally. Friends' or family's behaviors may be taken personally. In essence, the filtering aspect of our perceptions is related to the level of certain brain chemicals. Brain chemicals can get out of balance through genetics, long-term stress, trauma, or lack of personal, spiritual, emotional or physical care.

Suicide and the Gay/Lesbian Adolescent

As I have consulted the literature and have worked with youth who have sexual identity issues, there can be no denying that gay and lesbian youth are at a much higher risk for both attempts and completions of suicide. GLBT individuals appear to be at a higher risk for psychiatric illness, especially during the adolescent stages of their lives. In a 1993 study conducted by the American Academy of Pediatrics on gay and lesbian youth in America, it was concluded that these youth are at a "much higher risk" for many problems, including suicidal behaviors. This report also notes that, "Although data is warranting concerns by pediatricians, sexual orientation issues have generally been ignored by the mainstream researchers of teen suicide."[3]

The Risk Factor

It is commonly known by researchers of the suicide issue, that homosexually oriented individuals have been reported to be at a much higher risk since the end of the nineteenth century. Bell and Weinberg's 1978 study of 575 predominantly homosexual adolescent males and 284 predominately heterosexual adolescent males, matched on a basis of age, education, and occupational level, showed that gay males were 13.6 times more likely to have attempted suicide by age 21. A 1989 Department of Health and Human Services report entitled *Report of the Secretary's Task Force on Youth Suicide* estimated that GLBT youths might account for as many as 30% of youth suicides. 5 Safren and Heimberg (1999) compared 56 GLBT youths to heterosexual youths ages 16 to 21 and found that more than twice as many GLBT youths, (30%) compared with heterosexual youths (13%) reported a prior suicide attempt. 6 Twelve recent studies all show that adolescent gay males are at an increased risk. The Bagely and Tremblay data reveals that compared to heterosexual adolescents, gay, lesbian and bisexual adolescents were three times more at risk for a suicide attempt, but four times more at risk for a suicide attempt requiring medical attention. 7 It is also suggested in the literature that a significant suicidal risk factor exists in homosexually orientated youth who have experienced sexual abuse before the age of 17. 8

As we consult the research and see these disturbing statistics showing gay and lesbian youth at a much greater risk, we must realize this fact; they have only represented the youth who were willing to disclose their sexual orientation. Because of this fact, we must conclude that this problem is of a much greater magnitude than what is being reported. Research shows that gay and lesbian youth are at a higher risk for "suicide associated" risk factors such as eating disorders, substance abuse, relationship problems with the heterosexual population, etc. Unfortunately, most of these risk factors are carried over into adulthood.

What We *Can* Do

Given the gay and lesbian risk for suicide problems, especially adolescents, and the general lack of related knowledge and understanding in mainstream suicidology, a major education remediation effort is needed to begin effectively addressing the problem. A proactive stance rather than a reactive one should be taken for this at-risk segment of our population. We must make awareness a top priority as experts claim that suicide is the number one cause of death in adolescents with sexual identity issues. It is also extremely important to be on the lookout for bullying at school. These students are very vulnerable to the bullying of others. This can lead to a lack of self-esteem, deeper depression, a more fragile state of mind, and a greater sense of fear.

Major adjustments need to be made for intervention and prevention strategies focusing on reducing suicidal behaviors in gay and lesbian youth. Silence about gay and lesbian issues in suicide prevention programs can very well communicate the perception to gay and lesbian youth that no one will be able to understand them. The results may be catastrophic, and harmful consequences may result from intervention and prevention programs that either marginalize or do not address gay and lesbian issues in a respectful and understanding manner. Educators, community leaders, clergy and others should be aware that the situation exists and is an issue that needs to be addressed.

Suicide and the African-American Adolescent

While suicide was once relatively rare among African-American adolescents, a study released in May of 1998 by The Center for Disease Control in Atlanta is alarming, showing a dramatic increase over the last two decades. Males account for 84% of all suicides in the African-American population. 10

Answering The Cry for Help
© National Center For Youth Issues • www.ncyi.org • 1-800-477-8277
Please refer to page 2 for duplication information

When consulting professional counselors and clinical psychologists on this issue, there seems to be three common denominators:

1. *Feelings of not being wanted*
2. *Feelings of not having a place in society*
3. *A sense of alienation*

Many of these issues appear in combination for these adolescents. When you include substance abuse and the availability of guns, you have a bonafide potential suicide victim.

Many poor African-American adolescents see their lives as hopeless. Generally speaking, these adolescents come to school ill prepared for the learning process. Failure occurs and frustration grows. These feelings of hopelessness have caused suicide ideation in many of these adolescents, which may manifest to suicidal behavior.

The middle-class African American adolescent is in between the poor Black world and the White professional worlds. This puts him at risk for depression, alienation, and isolation from the mainstream of society.

I have also witnessed many well-meaning African-American parents of adolescents overreact to report card grades. A good education is viewed, (especially by African-American parents), as a vehicle out of poverty. When parents overreact, the balance is shifted from encouraging them to succeed to an unhealthy expectation level that they may not be prepared for, conflict is inevitable. When conflict occurs, a barrier to quality communication is created. When there is no quality communication between parent and child, there is usually no solution to the problem.

Too often, the adolescent who most needs professional counseling, be they White, Black, Hispanic, or Native American, has the least access to it. This is true especially for the poor African-American adolescent. When you look into the Black community, the biggest portion of which is poor, you don't see health care programs that can deliver the needed services. More often than not, guns are more readily available than treatment for these needy adolescents.

Suicide and the Hispanic Adolescent

In studying the Hispanic Adolescent and suicide in America, one concept stands out very clearly; "diversity." The American Hispanic youth is a very diverse population from a social, as well as a cultural standpoint, spanning from region to region in the United States. There are such great differences that it is hard to isolate symptoms different from other cultures. However, a close study of the literature reveals two influential concepts unique to the Hispanic adolescent; religion and family.

Most Hispanics view suicide as the "unforgivable" sin against God. They generally believe that a person who completes a suicide attempt goes to Hell. Although we know that fear is a short-term motivator, there is no denying that the church is a very powerful force within the Hispanic community. This confirms the fact we see in the literature, that the more religious a person is, no matter what faith or form it takes, a suicide attempt is less likely.

Many Hispanic adolescents come from a strong family-roots system. These strong family values and ties are part of a heritage developed in their emigrating country. Statistics show that Hispanics born outside the United States are at a lower risk for suicide than those that are American born. According to the Southwest Detroit Hispanic Community: "As Hispanics Americanize, they become more vulnerable to suicide." [11] A study conducted by the University of California claims, "The longer Hispanics are in the United States, the more susceptible they are to suicide, supporting the claim that coming from a strong family-roots system to a country with a weaker one can erode away at taught values and beliefs." [12]

There is no question that religion and family are major factors in the prevention of suicide for the Hispanic population of the United States. Dr. Orlando Villegas of the Detroit Public Health Department states, "…This is true 99 out of 100 times." However, if a Hispanic adolescent were suicidal, it would be rare if they talked to a friend, or talked to their teacher. The first person a Hispanic adolescent will talk to is a family member or the clergy." [13]

In a storm, **any** port will do. However, people who can relate on a cultural basis may be more effective because of common experiences and culture. This is not to say that a person from a different culture can't be effective. They certainly **can** be effective. **Care and compassion transcends all barriers of race, culture, and the socioeconomic status.**

Native Americans

Native Americans have traditionally had higher suicide rates when considering ethnicity factors. Tribes on reservations in the West and Northwest have adolescent suicide rates four times the national average. Tribes in the Midwest (although we don't know why) have suicide rates that are actually below their state averages. [14] However, the adolescent suicide rate for Native Americans is 1.5 times higher than the national rate. Men ages 15 to 24 account for 65% of all suicides among Native Americans. [15]

Ethnicity is a complex factor in determining suicidal risk. Great care and consideration must be given to racial heritage of potential suicidal persons.

24

© National Center For Youth Issues • www.ncyi.org • 1-800-477-8277
Please refer to page 2 for duplication information

Social and Cultural Factors

As we look at the following list of social and cultural factors, we can clearly make a connection between them and the rising suicide problem in our country today.

- *There are more guns in U.S. households than there are adults.*
- *Western culture glorifies violence.*
- *62% of men use guns to kill themselves.*
- *3 million children in the U.S. are abused and neglected.*
- *1 out of 4 women who attempt suicide have been raped.* [16]

Brain Chemistry and Suicide

The brain is the master processor of all emotions, thoughts, behaviors and muscle movements. It is no wonder with it's complexity that research emerges daily on factors that contribute to brain health and dysfunction.

One of the fundamental elements to understand in the brain is the area of neuro-chemistry or more simply, brain chemistry. Nerves contain breaks called synapses where these tiny chemical droplets transfer energy from one side of the broken nerve to the other. The level of chemicals as well as the type of chemical released will determine the end effect. For example, chemicals that slow nerve transmission will cause the slowing of other functions. These could include decreased muscle movement, increased alertness, hyper-excitability, scattered concentration or insomnia. Obviously, there is a fine balance that allows a person to operate most efficiently.

For years, physicians have used medication to change brain chemistry, therefore, changing behavior. Most notable in the educational arena is the medication for ADHD behaviors. This medication affects brain chemistry, which affects behavior.

In recent years much study has gone into understanding one brain chemical in particular, serotonin. Serotonin has been linked to several behaviors including obsessive-compulsive disorders, alcoholism, depression, suicide and violence. It appears that a deficiency of this particular chemical predisposes a person to these types of behaviors. This brain chemical alteration, coupled with inadequate coping mechanisms, may predispose a person to suicide or violence.

The question that arises is how does the brain become deficient of serotonin? There are three probable reasons. First, genetic or inherited issues may come into play. Many studies have shown the link between parental alcoholism, perfectionism, obesity, schizophrenia and other biochemical disorders that are somewhat independent of environmental factors, giving support to the theory that serotonin deficiency may also be genetically related.

© National Center For Youth Issues • www.ncyi.org • 1-800-477-8277
Please refer to page 2 for duplication information

Secondly, during the developmental years of a child's life, constant exposure to stress, anxiety or behaviors that alter biochemistry consistently may impact the young child's brain. For example, children from families with conflict during their developmental years are more likely to show depression later as adults. The child from a dysfunctional family often shows a grouping of behaviors that can be linked to biochemical alterations.

Finally, a person who is imbalanced in some area of their life can get out of balance biochemically. For example, Anorexia Nervosa is a disease characterized by inadequate nutritional support. This can lead to the negative effects of an altered biochemistry.

Another common situation that causes biochemical alterations is long-term stress. Out-of-control stress causes an increase in cortisol, the "fight or flight" chemical. Too much stress creates too much cortisol, which can cause many biochemical and physiological issues, such as elevated blood pressure, blood sugar imbalances, and the inability to let the body relax and rest.

Reports are beginning to surface which show that children with lower serotonin levels are more likely to be self-effacing and predisposed to suicide than non-chemically altered children. Additionally, if a second chemical, dopamine, is elevated, externally directed violence may also be more likely to occur.

Remember the relationship between altered brain chemistry or low serotonin, and changes in perception that were discussed earlier in Chapter 2. Individuals suffering from schizophrenia have an altered perception of reality. This same phenomenon happens when other chemicals are altered. Most individuals with brain chemical imbalances see themselves negatively, interpret all situations personally and develop a self-defeating behavior. It is important to correct the brain chemistry as well as provide counseling or insight. Please be aware that correcting brain chemistry does not imply that medication is the *only* approach. When chemical imbalances are present, both medication therapies as well as counseling protocols must be considered to bring about the most effective, positive, and healthy outcome.

Why Parents Have Gray Hair

A Father passing by his son's bedroom was astonished to see the bed nicely made up and everything neat and tidy. Then he saw an envelope propped up prominently on the pillow. It was addressed, "Dad." With the worst premonition, he opened the envelope and read the letter with trembling hands.

26

Dear Dad,

It is with great regret and sorrow that I'm writing you. I had to elope with my girlfriend because I wanted to avoid a scene with you and Mom. I've been finding real passion with Joan and she is so nice. I knew you would not approve of her because of her piercings, tattoos, her tight motorcycle clothes and because she is so much older than I am. But, its not only the passion dad, she's pregnant.

Joan says that we are going to be very happy. She owns a trailer in the woods and has a stack of firewood, enough for the whole winter. We share a dream of having many more children. Joan has opened my eyes to the fact that marijuana doesn't really hurt anyone. We'll be growing it and trading it with the other people in the commune for all the cocaine and ecstasy we want.

In the meantime, we'll pray that science will find a cure for AIDS so Joan can get better; she sure deserves it. Don't worry Dad, I'm 15 years old now and I know how to take care of myself. Someday, I'm sure we'll be back to visit so you can get to know your grandchildren.

Your Son,

Chad

P.S. Dad, none of the above is true. I'm over at Tommy's house. I just wanted to remind you that there are worse things in life than the report card that's in my top drawer. I love you! Call when it is safe for me to come home!

Moral of the Story – Keep things in Perspective!

Answering The Cry for Help
© National Center For Youth Issues • www.ncyi.org • 1-800-477-8277
Please refer to page 2 for duplication information

Endnotes – Chapter Two

1. A Mental Health Crisis Among Chinese Youth, Psychology Today, July/August 2008

2. Robertson, Joel, "Peak Performance Living" Harper-Collins, 1995.

3. American Academy of Pediatrics, "Risk Taking Behaviors Among Gay and Lesbian Youth"

4. Bell and Weinberg, "The Homosexual/Bisexual Factor on Male Youth Suicidal Behaviors," Third Regional Adolescent Suicide Prevention Conference, 1997.

5. Dept. of Health and Human Services, 1989

6. Safren and Heimberg, "Depression, Hopelessness, Suicidality and Related Factors in Minority and Heterosexual Youth." Journal of Clinical Psychology. 1999, 67, 859-866.

7. Bagely and Trembley, "Suicidality Problems in Gay and Bisexual Males," Ashgate Publishing LTD., Aldershot. England, and Brookfield Vermont, 1997.

8. Bagely and Trembley – **(same as above)**

9. Center for Disease Control, Atlanta, GA 1998

10. Granello and Granello, "Suicide: An Essential Guide for Helping Professionals and Educators." Pearson Publishing, 2007

11. Dr. Orlando Villegas, Mich. Assoc. of Suicidology Conference 1997

12. "Suicide in the Hispanic Population," University of California, 1995

13. Dr. Orlando Villegas, Michigan Assoc. of Suicidology conference, 1997

14. University of Minnesota, Klosk Study, 2003

15. University of Minnesota, Klosk Study, 2003

16. National Bureau Of Statistics, 2004

© National Center For Youth Issues • www.ncyi.org • 1-800-477-8277
Please refer to page 2 for duplication information

Chapter

3

Recognizing the Signs of Distress

Assessing Suicidal Risk

Chapter Three

Recognizing the Signs of Distress
Assessing Suicidal Risk

A student in your school approaches a staff member and informs him that her friend has been acting very strange. She goes on to say that this friend said, "I may kill myself." This scenario has occurred several times in my career and was not taken seriously. Unfortunately, in a few instances, the results were fatal. The point is *we have to consider all threats seriously*. Every school should have a protocol to follow when a situation such as this one arises and *every* staff member in the school should be aware of the protocol.

Sample Protocol

The following is just a sample of what your school protocol might look like in the event that a student verbalizes the intention or thought that he/she is considering suicide.

1. *Locate the student and have a staff member walk with him/her to the counseling office.*

2. *The staff member offers to stay with the student as the counselor speaks with the student in crisis. If the staff member is a teacher, locate a staff member on prep to cover this teacher's class.*

3. *The counselor speaks with the student and assesses the situation.*

4. *The counselor shares the assessment with the building principal. The student is not left alone during this time, but with a staff person.*

5. *Principal contacts parents.*

6. *Parents, counselor, principal and possibly the student in crisis will determine the course of action.*

7. *Log all steps taken and what was agreed upon. Keep on file in the guidance office.*

Remember, just as important as having an established protocol is that *every* staff person is aware of and understands the protocol and the reasons for it.

Recognizing an Individual in Suicidal Crisis

It is not always easy to recognize a person in suicidal crisis, especially the student who is on the honor roll, is well liked, and seems to have a bright future. These are the students that are always there for their friends and classmates. What we tend to forget is that these students have their down days as well. These students are also vulnerable to brain chemistry imbalance that may lead to depressive episodes. My experience has taught me that it is very difficult for these students to ask for help. The smarter they are the better they are at wearing the *"depression mask."* These are the students who are difficult to recognize. Most of the new Health Education curricula contain up-to-date lessons on depression, emphasizing that depression is

© National Center For Youth Issues • www.ncyi.org • 1-800-477-8277
Please refer to page 2 for duplication information

> Everyday in America there are honor students and seemingly well-adjusted teens taking their own lives. Don't overlook the honor student. Good grades don't necessarily equate to a good and peaceful life. Implementing depression education and screening for all students where depression is discussed will help teens be aware of their own tendencies and needs.

a medical condition and not a character flaw. Most curricula contain a depression-screening component that can be taken by the student to evaluate if they may be susceptible to depression. In my experience as an at-risk counselor, these students come forward as a result of being exposed to or one of their friends being exposed to these effective and relevant curricula. For additional information you can consult the following websites: *www.lexapro.com*- to learn more about depression symptoms and methods of treatment, and *www.revolutionhealth.com/drugs-treatments/rating.patient* to learn abut depression as a disease, screening tools, and other helpful information. There are several links you can visit from this website as well.

Signs of Crisis Situations

A majority of adolescents in crisis do exhibit signs that they are in crisis. Some of the signs to look for are:

1. *A poor self-image.*
2. *Antisocial behavior and isolation. They become introverted and withdrawn.*
3. *A drastic change in behavior and loss of interest in things the individual once cared deeply about.*
4. *Open threats or clues about ending their life. Clues may be found in writing assignments or art projects.*
5. *Excessive use of alcohol or other drugs.*
6. *A change in habits of appearance. A usually well-groomed adolescent begins to let his appearance go; appearance is usually an important issue for most teens.*
7. *Giving away prized possessions, especially for unknown reasons. Those in support groups have shared with me that they gave away possessions so they "wouldn't be forgotten."*
8. *Poor communication with family and friends.*
9. *A history of prior attempts of suicide. As mentioned before, every attempt seems to be easier and more dangerous.*

Telltale Signs

If you suspect that a person may be in crisis after assessing them from the list above, begin looking for more specific signs such as the following:

1. Scratching or superficial cutting, especially if the cuts go vertically up the arm. **If the cuts go up and down vertically, the person needs immediate professional help.** This pattern is very painful and is done to create physical pain to take the focus off his/her emotional pain. It is also more dangerous as it can cause dangerous blood loss in a short period of time.

2. A recent significant loss. It may be a death in the family, divorce, friend moving away, etc. The individual in crisis may not possess the resiliency skills to cope with the situation.

3. Themes of death or depression in writing, artwork or conversation.

4. Statements like "I'd be better off dead," or "Nothing matters," "I won't be a bother to you much longer."

5. Discord in the home which stirs up fear of abuse.

6. A sudden decline of academic performance.

7. Acute personality changes.

8. Feelings of helplessness and rejection.

9. Previous suicide attempt(s).

The SLAP Assessment

Although the **SLAP** Assessment does not take the place of a clinical assessment, it can serve as a guide for all who work with adolescents. **SLAP** is an acronym for the following:

S – How **Specific** is the plan. Ask what the plan is. The more specific the plan, the more serious the person is about following through with the suicide.

L – What is the **Lethality** of the proposed method? This is a question the adult usually can answer without asking the person in crisis.

A – Has the person in crisis **Acquired** the means? How **Available** is the means?

P – What is the **Proximity** of helping resources where the plan will be acted out? Helping resources can be defined as hospitals, police stations, EMS offices, or any location where help could respond quickly in the event of an attempted suicide. The seriousness of the attempt can be judged by the proximity or time it would take for someone to discover and intervene thus stopping the attempt. (e.g. if the person plans to attempt suicide in a remote area where no one might discover him, then the risk is very high that they are serious about completing suicide.)

Although the **SLAP** technique may not be a foolproof method in assessing suicidal risk, it can give you a very good indication about how serious the teen may be about suicide. Once again, it does not take the place of a clinical assessment.

Answering The Cry for Help
© National Center For Youth Issues • www.ncyi.org • 1-800-477-8277
Please refer to page 2 for duplication information

I strongly suggest however that if a teen approaches you stating that he is thinking about suicide that you take them seriously, even if they don't score significantly on the **SLAP** assessment. It will be very helpful to consult with at least one other knowledgeable adult. A second opinion may save a person's life and relieve your anxiety as well.

Robertson Risk Factor Assessment

The *Robertson Risk Factor Analysis for Violence and Suicide* (pages 82-84) is a simple tool to help a person assess an individual's predisposition to violence toward themselves and others. This tool combines various familial, psychological, personality and sociocultural factors to help identify these risk factors. The general assessment will lay the foundation to determine violence directed towards self and others. The specific assessments are helpful to determine suicidal or violent tendencies.

Prevention Tips

In making suicide prevention a major emphasis of this work, I need to stress the following points:

1. **Removal of guns from the home** – *Impulsivity tends to be a dominant personality factor in adolescents. Removing guns will make it less likely for teens to act on impulse. Many avid hunters are very likely to resist this tip, so my plea to them is to keep hunting firearms under lock and key, keep ammunition out of the home, and/or keep firing pins in a separate place under lock and key. Most teens that complete suicide use firearms. Removing them has many times prevented a suicide.*

2. **Early detection of substance abuse** – *Many times, substance abuse is the result of unmet needs in a teen's life. The reason **why** the teen is using drugs is an issue that must be addressed. What needs are they trying to fill by using drugs? How can adults identify and help the teen satisfy these unmet needs? The earlier these issues are addressed, the more effective we will be in helping the teen get his life in order.* **Substance abuse is one of the leading causes of suicide at all age levels.**

3. **Family therapy for families experiencing multiple stressors** – *Many times the parent(s) forget or don't realize that they also need therapy or professional counseling in helping them deal with their suicidal teen. They send the teen to counseling, thinking the counselor or therapist can "fix" the problem. The teen in crisis will have a better chance to recover if parents and counselor work together to improve the living environment of the teen and gain greater insight into the life of their troubled teen.*

It is also important to note that most of the time, a healthy teen will not attempt suicide just because a friend did. The teen at risk is the teen that was at risk before the incident occurred. This is especially true for teens that are:

- *Abusing alcohol or other drugs*
- *Being abused or neglected by parents*
- *Experiencing family stress*
- *Experiencing a series of frustrating events in their lives*

Practice Suicidal Assessment

Practice assessing suicidal risk. Using the scale below, rate each of the following situations 1 to 10 with 1 being not likely to complete a suicide and 10 very likely to complete a suicide.

1	2	3	4	5	6	7	8	9	10

not likely   threatening   very likely

Situation 1

Rhonda – age 17 has two older sisters in college. One is studying law, the other medicine. Her mother works, and her father is an executive in a large company. As long as she keeps her grades up, her parents let her do most of what she wants. She seems to enjoy schoolwork because she spends so much time on it. She goes out with friends every now and then, but is most often off to herself.

Rating_____

Situation 2

John –age 18 is an honor student on his way to college. He is active in school clubs and organizations. Problems in John's home are common to most families under stress. Three months ago he and his girlfriend broke up. Lately, he has been having headaches and daydreaming a lot. He has dated other girls, but hasn't found anyone steady yet.

Rating _____

Situation 3

Julie – 15 years old, has many friends. When Julie's parents divorced five months ago, it was hard on her. She never mentioned suicide even though she was moody and pulled away from her friends. That is over with. Yesterday she came to school and happily gave away some of her CDs and books to friends just because she was "so happy now."

Rating_____

Situation 4

Jacob – age 17, is not athletic. The other day some of his teammates turned on him for losing their volleyball game. He is struggling with schoolwork. He causes no one problems and is not into alcohol or other drugs. He and his mother have been arguing a lot lately. His dad is on the road often. He does not want to go to college but hasn't told his parents yet because he knows they won't like it.

Rating_____

Answering The Cry for Help
© National Center For Youth Issues • www.ncyi.org • 1-800-477-8277
Please refer to page 2 for duplication information

What Happened

Situation 1

Completed suicide. Studying Rhonda's situation we can see these caution flags:

- *Youngest child, older siblings very successful, both parents work and may be less available than Rhonda needs them to be, few friends and lack of ability to share.*

Situation 2

Completed suicide. Studying John's situation we can see these caution flags:

- *Family under stress, break up in a relationship, headaches and daydreaming, which is indicative of unresolved conflict. A need to find a purpose and place in life –why the need to "go steady?"*

Situation 3

Completed suicide. Studying Julie's situation we can see caution and red flags:

- *Break up of the family, change in mood and withdrawal from friends, claims withdrawal period is over (which may mean she is suppressing the issues), and quick recovery (which may mean she has actually made the decision to go ahead with the suicide). Gave away prized possessions.*

Situation 4

Completed suicide. Studying Jacob's situation we see the following issues:

- *Feels he doesn't belong or fit in, family conflict, no role model from his father, frustrated with schoolwork and knows college will be harder but can't talk to his parents about not wanting to go to college.*

Most schools in the United States have students such as the ones we have studied. It is important that all school personnel have some training in recognition, assessment, and procedure. Also, schools and communities should have policies in place should a suicide occur. Appropriate prevention services should also be offered along with strategies in place so intervention can occur with people who pose a potential threat to their personal safety.

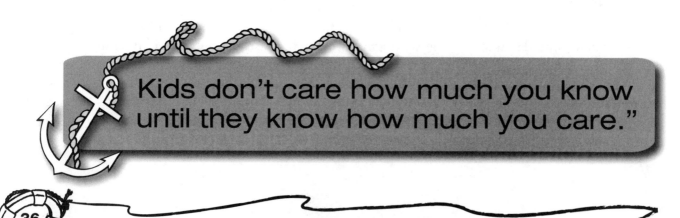

Kids don't care how much you know until they know how much you care."

Answering The Cry for Help
© National Center For Youth Issues • www.ncyi.org • 1-800-477-8277
Please refer to page 2 for duplication information

Chapter

4

Responding to the Call
Helping the Adolescent in Suicidal Crisis

Chapter Four

Responding to the Call
Help for the Suicidal Teen

"Suicide is not about death, it is about ending pain."

As stressed in the previous chapter, it is best to look upon any suicidal act, however lethal, as an effort by an individual to stop unbearable anguish or intolerable pain by doing something. Knowing this usually guides us as to the most effective way to help. In the same sense, the way to help save a person's life is to "do something."

Often letting others know about a person's struggles, breaking a promise to keep what could be a fatal secret, offering help, getting loved ones interested and responsive, creating action around the person that indicates concern, and offering caring compassion can prevent suicide. Many suicidal teens will inform a friend of his intentions to harm himself. It is of paramount importance that we teach teens not to keep these things confidential. The friend's job is not to counsel the friend in crisis, but to listen, and get them to a responsible adult. Also, we must stress that the friend in crisis *not* be left alone. If they won't go with the concerned teen to an adult for help, the friend can call 911 or send someone for help, but *do not leave the person alone*.

Guidelines for Helping a Person in Suicidal Crisis

If you are dealing with a person you think may be potentially suicidal, the following guidelines may be helpful:

- *Be up front. Ask the person if he/she is thinking about suicide. This might be the most single reliable way to find out if the person is really thinking about suicide.*

- *If the person answers "yes" to the above question, find out how serious he/she is. Start the SLAP technique mentioned in the previous chapter. Most people who haven't thought about how they will complete suicide will be disturbed by the first question, "What is your plan to do this?"*

- *If the person shares with you a very specific plan as to how they are going to carry out a suicide, do not leave this person alone. A crisis exists. This person needs to be assessed by a professional. Take this person to his/her parents (if the parents are understanding and willing to help), the county mental health clinic, or some other community resource. Make sure parents are notified and give them a chance to assist.*

- *If parents refuse to cooperate, inform them that their refusal in this circumstance is child medical neglect and that a referral will be made immediately to Children's Protective Services.*

- *If the person does not have a plan or yet acquired the means, but does have suicidal thoughts, a referral for counseling should be made.*

Answering The Cry for Help
© National Center For Youth Issues • www.ncyi.org • 1-800-477-8277
Please refer to page 2 for duplication information

In dealing with a potentially suicidal person remember the following points:

- **Be a good listener** – *Listen to not only what the person is saying, but also to what the person is telling you he/she can't tell you. Whenever I as a counselor do most of the talking, I do a lousy job of counseling.*

- **Evaluate the Individual** – *Does the person have a plan? Are they just emotional? Are they speaking in a rational way? Use the SLAP assessment.*

- **Don't suggest that they go and do it** – *How would you feel if they took your advice? Reverse psychology is not a good idea with suicide.*

- **Accept every feeling and complaint the person expresses** – *Don't argue with them, and don't confirm or encourage their actions or plans either.*

- **Be aware of fast recoveries** – *The person may just feel better because they made the decision to end his/her life. This can give a sense of relief. Recovery from these crises is a process not an event.*

- **Be supportive and affirmative** – *Give the person your assurance that everything possible will be done to help them.*

- **Help the person realize that a completed suicide is irreversible** – *You can't undo it. It will not change the situation. It has been said, "suicide is a permanent solution to a temporary problem."*

- **Remind them that depressed feelings can pass** – *Help the person realize there is someone who cares about them. Help the person realize that they do have a positive purpose in life. A potentially suicidal person usually doesn't want to hear clichés like "always stay with it," or "when the going gets tough, the tough get going."*

What To Do If a Person Seems Suicidal

Step One: Stabilize the Individual

- *Do not leave them alone.*
- *If they have a weapon, remove it if they will allow it.*
- *Move to a pre-arranged, non-threatening and isolated place.*

Step Two: Assess the Risk

Extreme risk – *won't relinquish a weapon*

- *Call police*
- *Keep the person calm by reassuring them*
- *Try to prevent him from harming himself*
- *Inform parents of any action taken*

Answering The Cry for Help
© National Center For Youth Issues • www.ncyi.org • 1-800-477-8277
Please refer to page 2 for duplication information

Severe Risk – *No weapon present but imminent danger*
- *Call Child Protective Services if distress is a result of parental abuse*
- *Call mental health agency if not parent abuse*
- *Take to the nearest hospital if unable to contact above*
- *Call parents to inform of action taken*

Moderate Risk – *Not imminent danger*
- *Call Child Protective Services if distress is a result of parental abuse*
- *Call parents to inform of action taken*

Step Three: Inform
- *Appropriate agency*
- *If other adolescents are present, inform them that their friend will be cared for*
- *Notify family*

Step Four: Follow-up
- *Log all procedures taken*
- *Determine if a referral has been arranged and is followed through*
- *Contact Child Protective Services if referral is not being pursued*
- *Monitor progress of the adolescent and make arrangements for the return to school*
- *Provide care, counseling and support services to those students or staff who are aware of or are involved in the adolescent's life*

What if a Student Threatens Suicide at School?

If any staff member becomes aware of a person threatening suicide, exhibiting self-destructive behaviors, or revealing suicidal thoughts through comments, writings, etc., the potential danger of this threat must be taken seriously. It has to be assumed that this person could in fact, act out his threat. I strongly suggest the school follow the established protocol suggested in Chapter 3.

If parents cannot be reached, the principal should call community resources such as county mental health, hospital, student's church minister, etc. If police have to be called, it is best to do this in as discreet a manner as possible. The Crisis Response team should be called upon to provide assistance to the staff, students, and the suicidal student's family as far as available community resources exist. The book *"Confronting Death in the School Family"* published by The National Center for Youth Issues is an extremely valuable resource for the development of your school Crisis Response team as well as being an important guide in the event that a suicide happen in your school or community.

The Guidance Department or school Crisis Response team should log all events and procedures and keep it in a confidential file. A copy of this report should be given to the superintendent of schools for informative purposes and confidential filing.

© National Center For Youth Issues • www.ncyi.org • 1-800-477-8277
Please refer to page 2 for duplication information

What if a Student Attempts Suicide on Campus?

If a person self inflicts an injury and the injury is perceived as life threatening, (bleeding, drug overdose, etc,) 911 should be dialed at once. The building principal should be notified (if unaware of the situation) and the following guidelines are suggested:

- *The principal should be prepared to give the name and age of the student and the nature of concern (I.e. injury or substance abuse). If substance abuse is present, give student's state of consciousness and save any evidence of the suspected substance ingested for Emergency Medical Services. (EMS)*

- *Place the student in isolation from other students and assign a staff member to stay with the student until the arrival of EMS.*

- *The student's parents should be contacted and directed to the medical facility where the student is being taken.*

- *The principal should write a follow-up report to the superintendent of schools and have a copy of this report for filing in the confidential file.*

- *As a follow-up, the family liaison of the crisis team will contact the family to provide assistance.*

- *Students who have attempted suicide on school property should not be allowed back in the school environment until clearance is received from a professional counselor or psychologist stating that it is safe for the student to return to school. This should be a policy approved by the Board of Education as part of the school crisis plan.*

Never leave the student alone in an acute crisis. If the student has made a plan and you feel they are serious, get help or leave them with a responsible adult while you go get help.

Components of an Effective School Program

Responsible schools, sensitive to suicide issues, have the following in place:

- **School crisis teams** – *Well trained with pre-crisis, crisis, and post-crisis phases of their crisis plan.*

- **School contact person** – *Designated to maintain communication among teachers and other school staff members, students, parents, and community treatment providers.*

- **Case Manager** – *Person who serves as a liaison between school and family, teachers, and the professional health clinic.*

© National Center For Youth Issues • www.ncyi.org • 1-800-477-8277
Please refer to page 2 for duplication information

- **Notification Procedures** – *Documenting referrals, notifying parents and working with depressed and suicidal students.*

- **Policies and Procedures** – *Clearly defined and appropriate steps to follow in the event of suicidal behavior and the responsibilities of the various school personnel in carrying out the plan.*

- **Training** – *For all school personnel.*

- **Provision** – *Provide positive information to students about the symptoms of depression and suicidal behavior, resources available in the school and community, and procedures for referring themselves or others to these services.*

Guidelines for Schools After a Suicide

When a suicide occurs, there is a fear others will follow the example and also attempt suicide. Schools need to be concerned about their role in responding to a suicide because of copycat suicides that have happened in several places across the country. The following is a list of suggestions for school personnel:

- *Consider how to respond to the death of a student or staff member **BEFORE** a tragedy ever takes place. The crisis response team should be chosen with plans developed for different situations in place with the approval of the Board of Education.*

- *Once the suicide occurs, the crisis response team needs to activate its plan as soon as possible.*

- *The students who were closest to the deceased should receive some additional time to help process the death. Having this group share what they knew of the deceased and any clues he/she may have shown will help answer to some extent the question "why." It also will help to begin to relieve some of the guilt and provide support from one another. It is particularly important to stress that one of the reasons the person took their life is that he did not talk about their feelings and problems. Encourage them not to make the same mistake.*

- *Provide an opportunity in the classroom for students and teachers to discuss their feelings about suicide. Stress that what they are feeling is normal. It is important to create an environment that is open and not critical of the feelings of others. Sample discussion activities can be found in Appendix B at the end of **"Confronting Death in the School Family"** published by National Center for Youth Issues.*

NOTE – Make sure the family liaison has permission from the family of the deceased to discuss the death as a suicide.

© National Center For Youth Issues • www.ncyi.org • 1-800-477-8277
Please refer to page 2 for duplication information

- *The Crisis Response team needs to express the fact that it is not only the peer group of the deceased that may become high risk. Students who have been troubled, depressed, or considered suicide, even though they did not know the deceased, may take the death personally. It may reinforce their feelings that the world consists only of problems and pain. The staff must be on the alert for the signs of a person in suicidal crisis.*

- *A month or so after the crisis, hold a meeting for parents to advise them of behaviors to watch for in their children, and inform them of available helping resources in the community should troubled behaviors occur.*

- *A month after the crisis, plan a presentation about general information on suicide for both teachers and students.*

- *Inform teachers that their student's stories, reports and drawings may hold clues of suicide intent. Many reported cases have shown this to be true and because of a lack of training as to the possibility of clues, they have gone either unnoticed or were passed off as insignificant.*

- *Provide opportunity in course offerings (Health Education, Social Studies, Language Arts, etc.) to teach about problem solving skills.*

- *Inform everyone that while guilt is a natural feeling after a suicide, the suicide was not his or her choice, it was the choice of the completor.*

Procedures for the days following a suicide

The following outline may be of help in the days after the tragedy of a suicide.

Day one

Announce the tragedy and follow your crisis plan, modify class schedules, and have teachers modify lesson plans. Set up and staff crisis rooms for students who need additional help after the classroom discussion activities. Also, follow the plan to aid the staff.

Day two

Attempt to get back to a regular schedule if possible. Follow up on students and staff who needed additional help on the first day. Staff must also take note of individuals who exhibit signs of needing additional help.

Day three

Although you will still have support available for students and staff, it is important to get back to a regular school schedule. Failure to do so can be counter-productive.

Day seven

Debriefing should take place for students and staff that exhibit signs indicating their need for assistance. *(See chapter six for more information on debriefing.)*

Answering The Cry for Help
© National Center For Youth Issues • www.ncyi.org • 1-800-477-8277
Please refer to page 2 for duplication information

Memorial Policy

Having a memorial policy in place before a tragedy ever occurs is extremely important for schools. There are many differences associated with handling death from an accident or illness versus death from suicide. The difference between the two should be carefully understood by the school and the school's crisis team. Notice the difference between the following lists:

Memorial Guidelines for Death Due to Accident or Illness

- *Provide a moment of silence in the deceased's honor.*
- *Flag may be flown at half mast.*
- *Encourage students to memorialize the deceased if they so desire.*
- *Encourage memorials to celebrate deceased's interest(s) in life.*
- *Plant a shrub or tree in honor of the deceased.*
- *Memorialize the deceased in the yearbook.*
- *Make a memory box and present it to parents of the deceased.*
- *Create a scholarship in the the name of deceased.*
- *Encourage discussion on the cause of death.*

Memorial Guidelines for Death Due to Suicide

- *Do not announce the death over the school PA system.*
- *Do not conduct a moment of silence.*
- *Avoid school sanctioned tributes, memorials, or events for at least one year.*
- *Do not lower the flags at half mast.*
- *Close friends of the deceased who wish to remember the deceased in a special way should be encouraged to do so in a quiet way that celebrates life. (Purchase a video on suicide prevention, collection for Yellow Ribbon Program, a researched publication of a list of teen resources, etc.)*

Why the Difference?

Memorials are not advised for suicide because;

- *There is a potential risk of glamorizing or romanticizing the suicide.*
- *Students who feel unimportant may come to believe that suicide is a way to become important.* [1]
- *Memorials can increase the attractiveness of suicide as a solution to problems.* [2]

> The intent here is not to judge the person that completed the suicide or his family, but to prevent copycat suicides and to promote positive problem solving skills.

© National Center For Youth Issues • www.ncyi.org • 1-800-477-8277
Please refer to page 2 for duplication information

Supporting a Depressed Family Member

Dealing with a depressed teenager can be a very frustrating, self-blaming, and confusing experience for parents. The following list is to help in these tumultuous situations:

- *Try to maintain as normal a relationship as possible.*
- *Acknowledge that the person is suffering.*
- *Don't expect the person to "just snap out of it".*
- *Encourage efforts to get treatment and get better.*
- *Express affection, offer kind words, pay compliments.*
- *Show that you value and respect the person.*
- *Help keep the person an active, busy family member.*
- *Don't pick on, or blame the person for his/her depressed behavior.*
- *Don't say or do anything that may worsen the person's poor self image.*
- *Take any talk of suicide seriously, and notify the person's health caretaker immediately.*

Advising Parents

Many parents have requested specific advice in the event their son or daughter talks of suicide. I suggest the following:

- **Listen** – *Encourage the teen to talk to you or some other trusted adult. Listen to the teen's feelings. Don't give advice or feel obligated to find simple solutions. Try to imagine how you would feel in the teen's place.*
- **Be Honest** – *If the teen's words or actions scare you, tell him. If you're worried or don't know what to say or do, say so. Don't be a cheerful phony.*
- **Share feelings** – *At times everyone feels sad, hurt, or hopeless. You know what it's like; share your feelings. Let the teen know he is not alone.*
- **Get Help** – *Professional help is crucial when something as serious as suicide is considered. Help may be found at a suicide prevention or crisis center, community mental health, or through clergy. Also become familiar with the suicide prevention program at the teen's school. Contact the appropriate person(s) at the school.*

Parent/Teen Conflict

In most American homes where teenagers exist, there is likely to be conflict between parents and teens. Conflict can be a barrier to communication between the two. When this situation exists, the parent needs to assess the situation and not necessarily give in, but avoid fighting. Agreeing to disagree is a very important ingredient in effective communication. The following list of suggestions is provided to help parents in the relationship process with their teen.

Parent/Teen Conflict Resolution Do's and Don'ts

Do	Don't
Bury the hatchet. Agree to disagree.	Fight and end all hope of resolution.
Reassure them that they have what it takes to handle life's tough times.	Micro-manage or run your teen's life.
Advise them when asked.	Pressure your teen to make the decisions you want them to make.
Have the courage to say "NO".	Refuse to cooperate.
Let them experience the consequences of their own decisions.	Run to their rescue at every turn.
Listen to your teen, give them choices, and invite their input and ideas. Add your thoughts, but agree to disagree when a compromise cannot be reached.	Do all of the talking or demand that they agree with you on every point.
Admit your own mistakes and what you've learned from them.	Portray that you were the "perfect teen."
Let them know you support them and believe they are capable of making right decisions.	Say, "I told you so" when they make mistakes.

Our youth really don't want to die; They just want their pain to go away.

Answering The Cry for Help
© National Center For Youth Issues • www.ncyi.org • 1-800-477-8277
Please refer to page 2 for duplication information

Suicidal Behavior Reporting Guide & Parent Release Forms

The forms found in the Appendix (pages 80 & 81) are to be used to document incidents and patterns of suicidal behavior of students. The parent release form documents the school's efforts to inform and assist parents in dealing with their children's behavior. Make use of these forms as you assess, report and communicate with parents and your Crisis Response Team members.

Major Recovery Issues

In helping the suicidal teen in the recovery process, the anticipated outcomes of the counseling professionals are as follows:

- *To get the teen to normal functioning as quickly as possible*
- *To help the teen regain control*
- *To help the teen establish his sense of equilibrium*
- *To help him re-establish a sense of trust*
- *To help him regain hope*

Deterrents to Risk

Research and experience clearly reveal that religion and family structure are the two most effective deterrents to suicidal thoughts and behaviors. There is no question to most people who work with teens that if teens have a spiritual identity, no matter what religion, they usually have a better outlook on life and more developed social skills in dealing with their problems.

Family structure is another important factor that reduces suicidal thoughts and behaviors in our youth. Whatever the family structure looks like, if it has a strong leadership and value system, the teen will be better equipped to handle the problems of life.

A successful strategy for counselors, other school personnel and community volunteers, is to identify and build on the developmental assets of our youth. These assets are the positive influences, relationships, environments, values, etc. that children are exposed to and may possess. The greater the number of such positive resources in a child's life, the more resilient they are to negative situations and events that they may face.

The Search Institute has identified 40 developmental assets that help our youth grow into emotionally healthy people. These assets include things such as participation in school, church and community activities (external assets), having a positive adult role model outside the family, and having loving involved grandparents and/or other extended family. A complete list of the assets may be found on the Search Institute's website. The successful school and community will identify these assets and build on them instead of concentrating on the negative. Research clearly shows that the more developmental assets a young person has, the less likely he will be involved in risk taking behaviors. Read more about the studies conducted by the Search Institute at www.search-institute.org.

© National Center For Youth Issues • www.ncyi.org • 1-800-477-8277
Please refer to page 2 for duplication information

The Power of Assets Against Risk Taking Behaviors

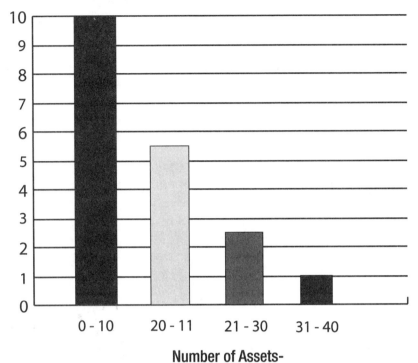

Number of Risk Taking Behaviors

(Such as drug abuse, negative social behaviors, educational / learning issues, etc.)

Number of Assets-

(Positive family and social influences and environments that help establish morals, values, etc. They help youth overcome negative situations and events that they may face.)

Developmental Assets and Risk Taking Behaviors

Of utmost importance is a quality and relevant substance abuse prevention program in the school and community. Research clearly shows that substance abuse is a major factor in both suicide attempts and completions.

Quality educational programs must also include input from students as well as parents and educators. Relevancy must be established for *every* lesson in the substance abuse prevention curriculum. Methods of delivery of information must be continuously evaluated and updated to relate to adolescents in the context of their world.

Police departments, churches, businesses and government must join hands with the school's substance abuse prevention program in a united effort of prevention.

A quality substance abuse education program must also have a solid parent component. This parent component must give pertinent information to parents, help with effective communication about drugs to their children, and encourage communication networks among parents for pledging drug free homes for their children and their children's friends who visit their home.

An effective substance abuse program must unite all agencies within the community to fight against substance abuse and provide quality life-changing education for both teens and parents.

© National Center For Youth Issues • www.ncyi.org • 1-800-477-8277
Please refer to page 2 for duplication information

49

Two Little Boys

A couple had two little boys ages 8 and 10, who were excessively mischievous. They were always getting into trouble and their parents knew that, if any mischief occurred in their town, their sons were probably involved.

The boys' mother heard that a clergyman in town had been successful in disciplining children, so she asked him if he would speak with her boys.

The clergyman agreed, but asked to see them individually. So, the mother sent her 8-year-old first, in the morning, with the older boy to see the clergyman in the afternoon.

The clergyman, a huge man with a booming voice, sat the younger boy down and asked him sternly, "Where is God?" The boy's mouth dropped open, but he made no response, sitting there with his mouth hanging open and wide-eyed. So, the clergyman repeated the question in an even sterner tone, "Where is God?" Again, the boy made no attempt to answer. So, the clergyman raised his voice even more and shook his finger in the boy's face and bellowed, *"WHERE IS GOD?"*

The boy screamed and bolted from the room, ran directly home, slamming the door behind him. When his older brother found him, he asked, "What happened?"

The younger, brother gasping for breath, replied. "We are in *BIG* trouble this time, dude. God is missing and they think *WE* did it!"

Moral of the Story-

Communication is critical for understanding and tackling problems.

End Notes- Chapter Four

1. Elder, Grolman, Wilson Institute for Adolescent Studies

2. Catone et al, "Research on Memorial Services for Suicide Completers", 1991

3. Robertson, J. Risk Factors for Violence and Suicide, Robertson Research Institute, 2002

4. Zajec, S. "The Michigan Model for Comprehensive School Health Education with the Search Institute's Forty Developmental Assets", Michigan Dept. of Community Health

Chapter 5

All Hands On Deck

Getting Parents and the Community Involved

Chapter Five

All Hands On Deck
Involving the Community

Someone once said, "It takes an entire village to raise a child." This wise person realized not only the different influences the child receives from the world (positive and negative) around him, but also the benefits of a "team effort" in supporting important core values vital for a quality life. Suicide prevention must be a community effort, not an isolated effort by the local school, church, or other institution. It is my belief that a "team effort" can make the difference in making a suicide prevention program a "mildly effective" isolated program into a "very effective" community program.

Community Suicide Prevention Coalition

The effective community suicide prevention coalition will get as many agencies involved as possible and target suicide prevention for all people of all ages in the community. Examples of these agencies include but are not limited to the following:

- *Schools: Superintendent, Student Assistance Coordinator, Middle and High Counselors, Teachers, Social Worker, and Students.*
- *City Council Officials*
- *Police Department Representatives*
- *Fire Department Representatives*
- *Youth Agency Representatives*
- *Community Mental Health Representatives*
- *Suicide Related Groups such as Survivors of Suicide Support Group*
- *Service Club Representatives*
- *Local Clergy*
- *Parents and Volunteers*

Working Together

In the first meeting of the coalition, the extent of the problem should be laid out for all to see. Your County Health Department will most probably have up-to-date statistics for anyone who may wish to see them. The major goal should be clearly defined and discussed. This goal may look like the following:

Reduce the incidence of suicide attempts and deaths for all age groups in the community

It is important to enlist help from other communities who have suicide prevention coalitions and plans in place. Use these plans to customize your goals and plans to your community's unique needs.

© National Center For Youth Issues • www.ncyi.org • 1-800-477-8277
Please refer to page 2 for duplication information

As your coalition continues to meet and evaluate needs of the community, more goals can be established. The suicide prevention coalition I serve upon discussed four areas of emphasis:

• Prevention   • Intervention   • Awareness   • Methodology

Under each area of emphasis we developed our goals. The following is an illustration of how we accomplished the task:

Prevention

- *Reduce the incidence of suicide attempts and deaths for all age groups*

Awareness

- *Develop broad based support for suicide prevention*
- *Promote awareness and reduce stigma*

Intervention

- *Develop and implement community-based suicide prevention program*
- *Promote efforts to reduce access to lethal means and methods of suicide*
- *Improve recognition and response to high risk individuals*
- *Expand and encourage utilization of evidence-based approached to treatment*
- *Improve access to mental health and substance abuse services*

Methodology

- *Improve and expand surveillance systems*
- *Support and promote research on suicide and suicide prevention*

Goals of an Effective County-wide Suicide Prevention Coalition:

1. *Reduce the incidence of suicide attempts across all age groups*
2. *Develop a broad based support for suicide prevention*
3. *Promote awareness and reduce the stigma*
4. *Develop and implement a community-based suicide prevention program*
5. *Promote efforts to reduce access to lethal means of suicide*
6. *Improve the recognition and response to high risk individuals within the community*
7. *Expand and encourage utilization of evidence-based approaches to treatment*
8. *Improve access to mental health and substance abuse services*
9. *Improve and expand surveillance systems*
10. *Support and promote research on suicide and suicide prevention.*

Your committee may take on all the above goals, or select just a few depending on the variables that exist in your community.

© National Center For Youth Issues • www.ncyi.org • 1-800-477-8277
Please refer to page 2 for duplication information

In the next step we used the Logic Model (blank planning sheet on page 79) to define the process of how we might reach our goals. The following is an example we used for each goal. Goal number one is used here as an example:

Goal: Reduce the Incidence of Suicide Attempts and Deaths Across All Age Groups

Objective	Action	What	Who	When
Broaden Public Awareness of Suicide Risk Factors	Develop Broad-based Support for Suicide Prevention	Advertising Prevention Programs and Marketing	Yellow Ribbon	
	Promote Awareness and Reduce Stigma	Fill Loop-holes in Early Treatment Awareness	Michigan Works	
		Suicide Clearinghouse	Faith-based Organizations	
		Educate about Documentation	Schools	
		Speaker's Bureau to Educate	Community Organizations	
		Faith-based Education Program	Healthcare Providers	
		Cross Trainings	Legistlators	
		Parent Education Helpline	Law Enforcement	
		Identify and Educate At-risk Individuals	Unions	
		Communication with All 24-hour Resource Centers	Caregivers	
		Suicide Prevention Coalition Buttons	Students Against Drunk Driving	
		Community Event Calendars	Saginaw Survivors of Suicide (S.O.S.)	
		Medical Coverage (Success and Survivor Stories)	Social Workers	
		Reach Service Organizations	School Counselors	
		Make Community Aware of Suicide Issues		
		New Audiences to Share Suicide Issues With		
		Health Fairs		
		Community Events for All Ages		

© National Center For Youth Issues • www.ncyi.org • 1-800-477-8277
Please refer to page 2 for duplication information

For every goal we developed a chart such as the one on the previous page. The time frame for the completion of the plan was just over a year of weekly meetings. It is important to keep the meeting time to no more than 90 minutes, because if the meetings go too long attendance will dwindle. It is imperative that you get all or as many key players (police, health care providers, faith based organizations, etc.) in your community involved as possible. The community effort is far more productive than an isolated effort by one well-meaning and motivated organization. Also, a community program has a much better chance of receiving funding for this large undertaking.

Suggested Sub-committees of the Coalition

- **Website Committee** – *Responsible for the development of the website*

- **Funding Committee** – *Researches and develops a full breakdown of funding opportunities*

- **Public Relations Committee** – *Responsible for informing the community about the Suicide Prevention Plan*

- **Education and Training Committee** –*Responsible for the education and training of the community about suicide prevention.*

Funding

A large undertaking such as this will need funding to implement the programs and activities necessary for success. There are grants that may be available at the state and federal level. One resource you do not want to overlook is the funding you may be able to receive from your own county. Various clubs and organizations should be solicited (such as Lions Club, Jaycees, etc.) along with businesses in the county. Asking businesses to provide representatives to serve on the coalition may be helpful in getting financial support for your efforts. The earlier you can start soliciting and securing funding, the easier the planning for the coalition.

Media Liaison

The coalition should appoint a media liaison to solicit help from the media in the form of positive publicity to the proactive approach of the coalition. There is no doubt that the media can be of great help to the coalition. The media liaison should be the contact person concerning upcoming activities and getting them announced over media outlets.

Students

I suggest that students from the local middle, high schools and colleges be involved on the coalition. Students are great resources for keeping the coalition realistic, and they usually have a good measure of energy. According to John Santrock, author of Adolescent Psychology, "Adolescents are the most energetic and dependable community service volunteers in the country."[1]

Answering The Cry for Help
© National Center For Youth Issues • www.ncyi.org • 1-800-477-8277
Please refer to page 2 for duplication information

Yellow Ribbon Program

The Yellow Ribbon Suicide Prevention Program is a proactive, preventative outreach program that distributes yellow ribbon cards and gives presentations and seminars promoting suicide awareness and prevention. These events are held for schools, church youth groups and organizations. The presentations address prevention of suicide as opposed to the many programs that are post suicide.

The Yellow Ribbon Suicide Prevention Program is already in place in numerous communities across the United States. The results reported have shown this program to be very effective in prevention for all ages. For more information about the Yellow Ribbon Program, you may contact:

Light for Life Foundation of America

P.O. Box 644

Westminister, CO 80030

FAX (303) 426-4496

Email: light4life@yellowribbon.org

Website: www.yellowribbon.org

Summary

Important components to keep in mind when developing your community prevention model are:

- *Promoting awareness*
- *Prevention*
- *Intervention*
- *Post-vention – School/Community crisis team training/staff training*

End Notes - Chapter 5

1. Santrock, John, "Adolescence" 12th edition, McGraw Hill, 2007

Chapter
6

HELP!

Navigating Through the Storm
*Working With Survivors
of a Loved One's Suicide*

Chapter Six

Navigating Through the Storm
Working with Survivors of a Loved One's Suicide

After doing a great deal of research on grief from deaths other than suicide, I have to acknowledge that I have learned about grief from suicide mostly from the survivors I have worked with in my experience as an at-risk counselor and SOS support group facilitator. I firmly believe from these experiences that suicide compounds the already difficult grief process. Some differences in the grief process after suicide and grief from death other than suicide include:

- **Perceived rejection** – *Survivors often see the suicide as rejection.* (1)

- **Violence of the death** – *Suicide deaths tend to be more violent and gruesome. The survivor usually experiences trauma, especially if he finds the deceased. Unless the trauma is dealt with, the grief process cannot move on. Survivors may need to restate many times over what they saw, heard, and experienced, etc. The listener must be patient. It may take several repeats for the survivor to process the experience. The skilled listener will guide the survivor to talk about the person and the good memories, not just the suicide.*

- **Societal taboo/shame/ostracism** – *Many times members of survivor groups have talked about being avoided by friends and neighbors after the suicide. Students who have experienced a suicide in their families report losing friends because their friends' parents won't allow them to associate with them. Suicide survivors need and want support after the death. They don't need to be made to feel like they have the plague.*

- **Blame** – *Either self-blame or blame of others. Both are very unhealthy. The skillful counselor impresses upon the survivor that it was the deceased's decision to complete suicide, not the survivor's.*

- **Suicide is less understood** – *Survivors are often alone in their grief because suicide is not frequently understood.*

- **Guilt** – *Guilt about not recognizing the signs or not helping when behavioral clues manifested.*

- **Anger** – *Anger toward the person who died. Many survivors are especially enraged by their certainty that the one who took his life wanted to cause them pain. In working with depressed individuals who made previous suicide attempts, they taught me that their inner pain was so intense they were not able to think about who they may hurt by their actions. They state that they could only focus on their inner pain.*

The Debriefing Process

The debriefing process following the suicide can be of great benefit to the surviving family and friends of the deceased. The following is a short outline of the debriefing process:

- *To help the survivor accept the tragedy emotionally as well as intellectually*
- *To recognize the individual who may need additional help*
- *To help the survivor understand the grieving process*
- *To prevent potential copy-cat suicides*
- *For growth to occur as a result of the tragedy*

Philosophy of Debriefing

Debriefing is the process by which the facilitator helps the surviving victims to clarify their thoughts, feelings and attitudes towards the crisis and the completor. It is the process of putting the incident and the individual's reactions in perspective. It is a group process designed to mitigate the impact of the event and to accelerate normal recovery. (Mitchell, 1991) The goals of this session are to acknowledge the situation, prevent trauma and provide hope. (2)

Purposes of Debriefing

The debriefing process is designed to prevent unnecessary complications that follow from exposure to tragedy. The goal is to prevent the formation of Post Traumatic Stress Disorder. In the process, the facilitators try to help the participants identify what happened and the role they may have played in the incident, and to discuss their emotional reactions and cognitive behavioral reactions to the experience. The group facilitators will also strive to identify issues and support needed in the future for the participants, and to refer for professional help if needed.

Who Needs Debriefing?

Debriefing usually occurs after a classroom or group defusing session has taken place. Not everyone will need to be debriefed, only those that are most exposed to the situation, those who had a close relationship to the deceased, or have similar issues as the completor. These may be witnesses, those who found the deceased, those otherwise involved with the situation or deceased, and of course, family members. Be on the lookout however for any individual who shows signs of inappropriate grief reactions.

When Does Debriefing Need to Take Place?

Use a defusing activity to determine who will need debriefing. Defusing activities can be found in the book *"Confronting Death in the School Family,"* published by The National Center for Youth Issues. Debriefing can be initiated 36 to 72 hours after the incident. After the incident, it takes time to identify those who need debriefing. The Crisis Response Team needs to make an impact list of students and staff most exposed or showing signs of needing additional assistance. The advantage of waiting a few days is that it is easier to evaluate the overall reaction and stability

Answering The Cry for Help
© National Center For Youth Issues • www.ncyi.org • 1-800-477-8277
Please refer to page 2 for duplication information

of all involved. This also allows time for the group facilitators to acquire important factual information and provides an opportunity for individuals to rely on their own coping skills to better determine for themselves the need to be involved in the debriefing process. There are some individuals who may show signs of needing debriefing a week after the defusing activity as the shock of the incident wears off into the realization that it actually happened. Your crisis response team should be prepared to provide assistance for these individuals.

Remember, debriefing is not a classroom activity. The suggested number of participants should not exceed 10. Each participant will be asked to respond to scripted questions and with groups larger than 10, the process will last too long and participants will become too exhausted to respond from a cognitive perspective.

Specific Incidents That May Require Debriefing

The following is a list of specific incidents that may require debriefing:

- *Floods*
- *Workplace/school violence*
- *School bus accidents*
- *Sudden death*
- *Hostage situations*
- *Hurricanes*
- *Fires*
- *Suicides*

It is important to remember that not everybody exposed to these incidents will need debriefing. Debriefing is for those *most exposed* to these incidents. Most exposed can mean the following:

- *Surviving victims, including those involved in the incident*
- *Witness to an accident*
- *A relation to the victim of the incident*
- *Verbal exposure – listening to the details of a traumatic event*
- *Finding the deceased person*

Debriefing is more cognitive in nature than sensory. Many experts claim that it is far too cognitive a process for young children. My experiences strongly agree with these experts.

Defusing Vs. Debriefing

To explain the difference between defusing and debriefing, the following chart will prove helpful:

Debriefing	Defusing
Only for those most exposed	For all classroom children
Groups of 8 to 10 people	Groups of 20-30 people
Not for young children	Better with young children
Initiated 3-7 days after incident	Initiated day of or first day after incident
Done by trained outside consultants	Done by classroom teacher

The goals of defusing and debriefing are the same. Defusing is a sensory process while debriefing is a cognitive process.

Who Does the Debriefing?

Only trained professionals from outside the immediate trauma location (not within the school itself) should do the debriefing. The Institute for Trauma and Loss in Children regularly hold training sessions to certify professional debriefers throughout the country. They have a list of certified people who may live in your area. You can visit their website at www.tlcinstitute.org. It is best to have at least two debriefers for each group session.

Pitfalls of the Healing Process

Healing after the suicide of a loved one is a long, difficult process for most people. It seems to be a "two steps forward, one step backward" process. Difficulties that may be encountered during the healing process are as follows:

- ***Anniversary reactions*** – yearly, monthly and even weekly. The anniversary of death is a frequent stimulus for depression. Anniversaries of this event stimulate the painful awareness that a loved one is gone.

- ***A feeling that nothing else matters*** – The danger of blaming all the unhappiness felt on the suicide. It becomes a convenient excuse for not having to deal with other problems.

- ***Substance Abuse*** – Hiding from the pain will not bring about growth and healing. Grief is not the problem, it is the solution. Unfortunately we have to hurt to heal. Postponing facing the pain prolongs and may complicate the grief process.

- ***Ignoring One's Health*** – During the shock, it is common for people to neglect their own well-being. Sleep disturbance and loss of appetite cause the body to become run down. The survivor is especially vulnerable to physical illness.

- ***Milestones*** – Normal changes that occur may also reverse the progress being made toward recovery. Change is associated with growth and loss. Graduations, weddings, etc. mean moving on to something new while giving up something in the past. Each new step in the survivor's life moves them further away from the experiences they shared with the deceased. [3]

64

Answering The Cry for Help
© National Center For Youth Issues • www.ncyi.org • 1-800-477-8277
Please refer to page 2 for duplication information

Moving Towards Healing

The old adage "time heals all wounds" is not necessarily true for survivors of suicide. I believe it is what we do with time that will actually lead to healing. This is an experience the survivor will never get *over*, but can get *through*. Healing the pain of a loved one's suicide requires sharing and caring. Sharing of feelings with family members, friends, counselors, pastors, etc. is of critical importance. The caring of people around the survivor that comes in the form of listening, understanding, non-judgmental mentoring is critical to the skillful rebuilding of the survivor's self esteem and continued healing.

Advice from Survivors

The following list comes from survivors of a loved one's suicide and is compiled from support groups and meetings with survivors at conferences. Most have come from adolescents. Their advice to us can be very helpful in understanding and supporting these individuals.

- *"Mention the person who died by name. Personalize our loss."*

- *"Use the words '**dead**' and '**death.**' This communicates to us that you are willing to be honest."*

- *"Be patient. If we cry, please understand and if we make you feel uncomfortable, we don't mean to."*

- *"Thinking of you" cards or notes on anniversaries or the dead person's birthday are greatly appreciated. It is comforting to know that you still remember and care."*

- *"If we have surviving children, please show them the compassion you show to us. There are times that we hurt so much that we are too fatigued to reach out to our children. Anything you can do to help them is greatly appreciated."*

- *"Please don't tell us, 'I know how you feel.' "*

End Notes - Chapter Six

1. Smolin, C., Guinan, J., "Healing After the Suicide of a Loved One," Simon and Schuster, 1993, New York, NY

2. Stelle, William, "Trauma Debriefing for Schools," The National Institute for Trauma & Loss in Children. 2005

3. Robinson, R., "Survivors of Suicide," Newcastle Publishing Company, 1989, Van Nuys, CA

© National Center For Youth Issues • www.ncyi.org • 1-800-477-8277
Please refer to page 2 for duplication information

Chapter

7

Safe In the Harbor
Developing and Facilitating
Support Groups

Chapter Seven

Safe In the Harbor
Developing & Facilitating Support Groups

Support groups can be an appropriate and effective way to help bereaved people heal. They offer a safe place for people to do the work of mourning, to find encouragement, to reconcile their losses and to find continued meaning for living. The support group can be for people who have attempted suicide and survived, as well as the survivors of a loved one's suicide. I have had separate groups for both in the past which has worked well for me. If both groups are together, a highly skilled and experienced facilitator must be in charge. The formation and make up of the group depends heavily on the ability of the facilitator and the support system in place in the school and community.

The Role of the Support Group

The following list helps to define the role of the support group:

- *To offer a safe place for people to do the work of mourning, encourage members to reconcile their losses and to go on to find continued meaning in life and living.*

- *To counter the sense of isolation that many experience.*

- *To provide emotional, physical, and spiritual support.*

- *To allow mourners to explore their many thoughts and feelings about grief in a way that helps them to be compassionate with themselves.*

- *To encourage members not only to receive support and understanding, but also to provide the same for others.*

- *To offer opportunities to learn new ways of approaching problems.*

- *To provide a supportive environment that can revitalize their zest for life.*

As group members give and receive help, they feel less helpless and become able to discover new meaning in life. Feeling understood by others brings down barriers between the grieving person and the world outside.

Getting Started

Starting a support group can take a great deal of time and energy. Many school counselors decide not to start groups because they realize the many details that must be attended to. The group facilitator should not try to do everything him/herself. Help and support should come from members of the prevention coalition committee discussed earlier in this work (see page 53). It is always better when a group of compassionate and caring people share the workload and also bring a variety of creative ideas to the process.

Support Group Guidelines

A blank reproducible planning sheet for creating Support Group Guidelines may be found in the appendix on page 85.

In getting started the following should be considered:

1. Decide on a group format

What kind of group will you provide? A "self help" format, or a "social group" format? In choosing the format, the strength of the facilitator and personality of the group should be considered.

2. Find a meeting place

Obviously, the best place will be a comfortable, safe place appropriate for creating a supportive atmosphere, neither too large or small, and preferably distraction free.

3. Establish the structure

You must also determine the structure of the group. Will it be "open-ended," meaning that the group members come and go depending on their needs? Or will it be "close ended," meaning that the group will meet for a specific number of days or weeks?

4. Determine the length and frequency of meetings

If you are working with teens, usually during the school day will be best. Many schools have "homeroom" or "advisory" periods which make ideal times for a meeting to take place. I have been successful meeting one day a week with the group and utilizing only the "homeroom" or "advisory" time periods.

5. Setting the number of participants

The number of support group members will be related to the kind and quality of interaction the facilitator desires. When groups get too large, the sense of safety and freedom to be verbally expressive diminishes for many people. For involved interaction, try to limit your group to no more than 12 members.

6. Creating Ground Rules

Through establishing group ground rules, you can create a safe place for people to mourn. Ground rules are also important to the facilitator's role as a leader. For example, should someone begin to verbally dominate the group, the facilitator intervenes by pointing out a ground rule that ensures members will have equal time to express themselves.

Sample Support Ground Rules

1. Respect and accept both what you have in common with others and what is unique to you.

2. Don't set a specific timetable for how long it should take you and others to heal.

3. Feel free to talk about your grief. However, if someone in the group decides to listen without sharing, please respect his or her preference.

4. Make every effort not to interrupt when someone else is speaking

5. Respect others' rights to confidentiality. Do not use names of fellow participants in discussions outside the group.

6. Attend each group meeting and be on time.

7. Allow each person equal time to express him or herself.

8. Avoid giving advice unless a group member specifically requests it.

9. Recognize that thoughts and feelings are neither right nor wrong.

10. If you feel pressured to talk, but don't want to, say "no". Your quiet contemplation will be respected by the group.

In dealing with confidentiality, (rule 5) the group facilitator should explain that there are times when they will break confidentiality, such as when a person threatens to harm himself or others. The facilitator may also ask for input from the group concerning other times it may be appropriate to break confidentiality. If confidentiality is to be broken by a group member, the group should be given the opportunity to be in on the decision as to how it will be handled. The facilitator should then remind the group that it is okay to be angry, but not okay to be mean. The group also will be instrumental, if given the opportunity, in establishing ground rules.

Facilitator Roles

The role of the facilitator is to literally "make easier" purposeful discussion about the grief journey of group members, as they help to create a safe place that allows mourners to reconcile their loss and go on to find continued meaning in life and living.

The specific tasks of the group facilitator are as follows:

1. Plan and lead group meetings.

2. Listen – the facilitator must model effective listening.

3. Model openness and caring.

4. Keep the group on task yet be flexible to related issues that may arise.

5. Guide the group through difficulties which may occur and respond appropriately to destructive behavior in the group.

6. Participate in training opportunities – many colleges or regional educational service agencies sponsor group facilitator trainings.

7. Follow up on members outside the group time.

8. Evaluate the group process – Do changes need to be made? Is the group achieving its purpose?

> ## The two most important qualities in an effective group leader are **flexibility** and the **ability to share responsibility**.

Sharing Responsibility

A co-facilitator is usually a good idea. Joint leadership can make for a richer support group experience for all involved. This allows for two distinct personalities to offer healing, support, and guidance, along with sharing all the administrative work and details that need to be attended to.

Flexibility

Being flexible is important because as the group evolves, some meetings may take a natural path without much direction from the facilitator. Sometimes the meeting plan, no matter how well planned, should be put aside if the group dynamic moves in a different direction.

The support group will be influenced by the unique personalities of the group members and the leadership style provided by the group facilitator. The most important thing the facilitator can do is evaluate the "safeness" of the group for people to mourn, share, and express their feelings. If the group is not moving forward, try to discern why members don't feel a sense of trust and safety.

The support group can help the grieving person move forward to develop a renewed sense of confidence and an ability to fully acknowledge the reality of the death, and the capacity to become involved with the activities of living.

Additional Points

Parent Permission
Parental permission is strongly suggested for students under the age of 18 who wish to participate in the support group. In many school districts, it is policy because of possible parent dissent and to prevent legal problems.

Closure
Support groups for teenagers should have a closing phase. The group facilitator should establish a closing date before the first meeting takes place. Studies show that if the group goes on indefinitely staleness usually occurs, countering the growth that has taken place. If a member has not progressed or is just starting to progress, give them the option to join the next group's session. In the closing phase, the group facilitator's responsibilities include:

1. *Acknowledge what growth needs yet to occur.*
2. *Reinforce positive changes and growth.*
3. *Assist members in setting realistic goals for their future.*
4. *Assist members in applying specific skills to everyday life.*
5. *Provide closure individually as well as for the group.*

Answering The Cry for Help

Remember, a support group's main goal is not to give therapy, but to give the person a supportive environment. In misery, people need someone to support them as they walk through it. The effective support group lets it members be who they are in a familiar environment and doesn't solve problems of the past, but helps people deal with them.

Activities

I hesitate to give a list of suggested activities for a support group because each group I have facilitated has been unique. What has worked well with one would have not worked at all for another. I strongly suggest that you read over chapter six of this work and construct your own discussion and group activities to fit the needs of your particular group. The book *"Understanding and Addressing Adolescent Grief Issues"* published by The National Center for Youth Issues has an Appendix which can be of help, but don't get tied down to a set program that will not allow you to meet the individual needs of your group.

Communication

While addressing a marriage seminar on communication, David and his wife listened to the instructor declare, "It is essential that husbands and wives know the things that are important to each other."

He addressed the man, "Can you describe your wife's favorite flower?"

David leaned over, touched his wife's arm and gently whispered, "Pillsbury® All-Purpose, isn't it?"

Moral of the Story – Don't assume to understand until you listen!!

Answering The Cry for Help
© National Center For Youth Issues • www.ncyi.org • 1-800-477-8277
Please refer to page 2 for duplication information

Appendix

Setting the Anchor

**The 10 Most Frequently Asked Questions
& Reproducible Forms**

The 10 Most Frequently Asked Questions about Suicide

Note: The following is a list of the ten most frequently asked questions about suicide that I get asked during workshops, parent meetings and student assemblies. Please don't feel compelled to totally agree with me but please consider my insights:

1. Why do you use the term "Complete Suicide" instead of "Commit Suicide?"

I learned from my support groups that when they hear the word "commit" they related that to their loved one committing a crime. They tell me people "commit" murder, bank robberies, etc. They say they are offended when people refer to their loved one as "committing" suicide. Completed is a more sensitive and appropriate term.

2. Won't I put ideas in kids' heads by talking about suicide?

The National Association of Suicidology adopted a statement at their 2001 national convention that "Suicide is a national health problem. The number one preventative measure is to talk about it." The willingness to address the issue is seen as admirable and is appreciated by most teens. One evening after I addressed 800 plus people in a community that had 10 adolescent suicides in a year, I walked into a restaurant and was immediately surrounded by about 20 teens who indicated to me that they were at the function. I asked them, "What was the most important thing I said all night?" They all said without hesitating, *"we want to talk about it."* The number one suicide preventative measure is not Prozac®, but to talk about it. In this day and age, teens are under tremendous pressure. They appreciate caring adults who are willing to help them tackle the tough issues of life, and suicide is obviously one of these issues.

3. If I am talking to a person who at the time seems to be suicidal, should I come right out and ask him if he is thinking about suicide?

YES. Whenever I asked a person if they were considering suicide, I sensed a great sigh of relief in the person. It was like they were saying "FINALLY, somebody is willing to talk to me about this!" Even when I prefaced the question with, "You know, I can't keep this confidential if you say 'yes'," it still didn't stop them.

4. There are so many adolescent suicides. What is wrong with today's kids?

You are asking the wrong question. It's not what is wrong with today's kids. It is what is wrong with society. Please don't lay the blame for the adolescent suicide epidemic on the adolescents. This is the wrong attitude. People with this attitude will most probably do more harm than good in working with suicidal people. Society isn't listening to their cry for help and doesn't know how to respond to this epidemic.

5. Isn't depression a result of a character flaw? Maybe if the person made better decisions they wouldn't be depressed.

Although I agree that bad decisions have negative consequences and depression may be one of them, it is well documented that depression is a medical condition caused by an imbalance of brain chemistry. When we look at depression as a medical condition instead of a character flaw, we develop the proper attitude in dealing with the depressed individual. This individual may be depressed, but they are still very alert to our attitude. *A positive attitude will be of paramount importance as we interact with the individual.*

6. How is grief from suicide different than grief from death of other causes?

Suicide is a sudden death which many times can induce trauma and traumatic reactions. It is in most cases a more violent death. There also tends to be more guilt and anger with survivors of suicide than death from other causes. I call it the "I could of, should of, would of" syndrome. These issues compound the grief process.

7. Can I scare kids out of suicidal thoughts?

NO!! Reverse psychology is a BAD idea. Think about this: You are depressed and you share your thoughts about suicide with a person who you think will help; he says back to you; "Just go and kill yourself." Instead of scaring you out of the suicidal episode, he just convinced you that "I am right. Nobody does care." Think of the remorse you would feel if this person in crisis took your advice.

8. I have read claims that some medications meant to prevent depression, can actually be a factor or cause of a suicide. Is medication dangerous?

I have seen medication as a positive component to treatment of depression and other behavior disorders. I don't have enough information to refute the claims of these reports, but medication has been critical to the treatment of many depressed teens I have worked with. These treatments have been proven effective when closely monitored under a doctor's supervision. I do want to emphatically state however, that medication is only one component of treatment. Counseling and therapy are also of critical importance as well as diet, activity, and exercise.

9. What are the most important things to teach teens while helping a friend in suicidal crisis?

I believe that there are two extremely important principles we can teach teens to help a friend in suicidal crisis: First is to not keep the friend's crisis a secret. This being said, we need to teach the helping teen to either go with his friend to a responsible adult for help, or if the friend won't go with him/her, go to a responsible adult with the information and have them promise to get help immediately. Will the friend in crisis be upset? Probably. But he will be alive and when he recovers he will realize the courage it took for his friend to break confidentiality and seek out help. The second thing we can do is teach them that if their friend is in an acute crisis, don't leave him alone until he is in the care of a responsible adult.

10. What have been some of the worst things that could be said to a teen in suicidal crisis?

The worst thing said would have to be the reverse psychology line of "just go on and do it." The others include the following:

- *"These are the best years of your life." When you tell a depressed person that they are currently in the best years of their life, what hope does he have for the future? You may very well be communicating that things will not get any better, or "toughen up and stop complaining." All things this depressed person does not need to hear.*

- *"You have your whole life ahead of you" – The depressed person may very well hear you saying that he has to be miserable for his whole life. Once again, the depressed person is not given any hope, only continuing discouragement.*

- *"If you think you have problems now, wait to you become an adult and have the pressures of raising a family, a job to go to and bills to pay, etc."*

Answering The Cry for Help
© National Center For Youth Issues • www.ncyi.org • 1-800-477-8277
Please refer to page 2 for duplication information

Sample Goal Worksheet for Suicide Prevention Coalition

Goal: Develop Broad-Based Support for Suicide Prevention

Objective	Action	What	Who	When

Answering The Cry for Help
© National Center For Youth Issues • www.ncyi.org • 1-800-477-8277
Please refer to page 2 for duplication information

Suicidal Behavior Reporting Guide

Student's Name	Date
Person Submitting Report	Grade
School	Birth Date

1. How did staff become aware of suicidal threat/action? _____
   _____
   _____
   _____

2. Describe incident and/or situation surrounding threat/action (personal difficulties, school problems, etc.) _____
   _____
   _____
   _____

3. What was the means used or threatened? (weapon, instrument, drug, other)
   _____

4. Lethality: Low _____ Medium _____ High _____

5. Designated staff person responsible for contacting parents. _____

6. Which family member was contacted? _____

7. Parent contacted: Yes _____ No _____

8. Parents response

   _____
   _____
   _____
   _____

Follow Up: Date: _____ Who: _____

Action:

   _____
   _____
   _____
   _____
   _____
   _____
   _____
   _____

Answering The Cry for Help
© National Center For Youth Issues • www.ncyi.org • 1-800-477-8277
Please refer to page 2 for duplication information

Parental Agreement/Release Form

Having met with member(s) of the Crisis Response Team and having discussed concerns
about my child _____
(child's name- please print)

regarding _____

I, _____
(parent's or guardian's name- please print)

Check one:

☐   Agree to cooperate and follow through with the recommendations made.

☐   Disagree with the recommendations made and take full responsibility for the
welfare of my child and any outcome of this crisis.

☐   Understand that the welfare of children is a shared responsibility and that if no
help is sought for a child at risk that state and federal laws require notification of
Child Protective Services for further investigation.

Parents/Guardian's signature _____

Principal signature _____

Crisis Response Team Representative signature _____

Follow Up _____

_____

Date: _____

Who: _____

Action: _____

_____

_____

_____

cc: Principal's Confidential File/Superintendent

Robertson General Risk Factor Assessment

GENERAL ASSESSMENT *indicates major issues that are of immediate concern	YES	NO
Withdrawn		
Perfectionism		
Poor impulse control		
Aloofness		
Aggression		
Lack of Trust		
Rigidity		
SOCIAL AND CULTURAL ISSUES		
Increased rates of violence w/decreased levels of concern*		
Changes in family structure		
Problems with friendships		
Increased mobility w/disruption of friendships and social networks		
FAMILY ISSUES		
Partnership dissolution		
New family relationships		
Inconsistent parenting		
Family history of physical or psychiatric illness		
PSYCHIATRIC OR PSYCHOLOGICAL HISTORY		
Personal history of depression, schizophrenia, or bipolar disorder		
Personal history of conduct disorder*		
BEHAVIORAL ISSUES		
Inappropriate use of alcohol, drugs, or solvents*		
Impulsive behavior and other conduct disorders, including rage, anger, & hostility*		
BIOCHEMICAL AND GENETIC FACTORS		
Reduced brain activity		
Reduction in serotonin*		
STRESSFUL LIFE EVENTS		
Physical abuse*		
Sexual abuse*		
Dysfunctional family system		

Copyright Robertson Institute LTD

Positive responses from General Assessment: _____

Answering The Cry for Help

Suicidal Risk Assessment

After completing the General Assessment, complete the Suicidal Risk and Violence assessments.

SUICIDAL RISK ASSESSMENT ★indicates major issues that are of immediate concern	YES	NO
Loss of control*		
Increased mobility with disruption of friendships and social networks		
Sexual identity issues (gay or lesbian)*		
Death of a parent, caregiver or another family member		
Suicidal behavior in the family*		
Prior attempts at suicide*		
Writing suicide notes and choosing suicide method		
Inability to tolerate praises or rewards		
Not wanting to be touched by others		
Apathy about dress or appearance		
Sudden changes in weight		
Variations in work performance or daily lifestyle		
Exposure to attempted or completed suicide*		

Copyright Robertson Institute LTD

The following is a general rule of thumb, but must **NOT** be considered diagnostic; rather it is provided for information purposes only.

- *Positive Responses from General Assessment*   _____
- *Positive Responses from Suicidal Risk Assessment*   _____
- *Total Positive Responses*   _____

Total Positive Response Score
(except sexual identity- a positive response here is moderate to high risk.)

0-6	7-12	>12
Mild Risk	**Moderate Risk**	**High Risk**

Violence Risk Assessment

VIOLENCE RISK ASSESSMENT	YES	NO
History of animal torture (7-8 years of age)		
History of expressions of violence i.e. blowing-up something. Expressing desire to kill someone.*		
Showing firearms to friends with or without threats.		
Feelings of loss of control, rejection, humiliation or isolation.		
Struggle with "fitting in".		
History of being teased or ridiculed.		
History of traumatic experiences, especially at home.		
History of getting in trouble on a routine basis.		
Communicates "killing" as opposed to "getting back at someone."		
Expresses he or she has access to a gun.		
Has a specific plan for how to commit a violent act*		
History of expulsion from or dropping out of school or social groups.		

The following is a general rule of thumb, but must **NOT** be considered diagnostic; rather it is provided for information purposes only.

- *Positive Responses from General Assessment*   _____
- *Positive Responses from Violence Risk Assessment* _____
- *Total Positive Responses* _____

Total Positive Response Score
(except sexual identity- a positive response here is moderate to high risk.)

0-7	8-13	>13
Mild Risk	**Moderate Risk**	**High Risk**

Answering The Cry for Help
© National Center For Youth Issues • www.ncyi.org • 1-800-477-8277
Please refer to page 2 for duplication information

Support Group Guidelines Planning Sheet

Refer to Chapter 7 (pages 69-73) for details about Support Groups. Use this sheet to plan your own personal Support Group.

1. Decide on a group format

_____

_____

_____

2. Find a meeting place

_____

_____

_____

3. Establish the structure

_____

_____

_____

4. Determine the length and frequency of meetings

_____

_____

_____

5. Set the number of participants

_____

_____

_____

6. Create Ground Rules

_____

_____

_____

© National Center For Youth Issues • www.ncyi.org • 1-800-477-8277
Please refer to page 2 for duplication information

Notes

Notes

Notes